ETERNAL TRUTHS

EVA MINOCHA

Made with ♥ on the Notion Press Platform
www.notionpress.com

Contents

Contents

Foreword

I began writing poems for some of my school projects and things like that .After sometime I thought of writing a book of my own in an undefined manner or undefined future. I just kept writing for pleasure and it soon turned into my dream. I wanted people to hold a book on which my name was written. I also got inspiration from some of my teachers and people of my age publishing their books .I thought that publishing is not a big deal at such young age too. I started sending my poems for small competitions and they gave me some self confidence. I gathered knowledge about the procedures and finally I am here WITH A BOOK WITH MY NAME !! During writing,I faced many hurdles. Midway through writings,I lost some of my favourite poetries. I tried to find them more than anything but couldn't. A little humourous but then I wrote poem relating to such failures and barriers!!Moreover during a period,I felt like what if these poems are not so good,what if they're too childish,what if anyone doesn't like them?Then,I wrote the poem SELF TRUST and told myself to go ahead,whatever will happen,we'll see!!

Acknowledgements

Hey everyone! A big thanx to all of you for giving me a chance by trying this book!! I would like to say that this book is really a result of mixtures of my hardwork, aspirations ,desires, ideas, thoughts etc. Thanx to my family and friends who encouraged and appreciated me. When three of my poems got published in three different books ,I was so happy with that and now I am publishing wholely and solely my own book !! A big dream come true!! I hope your support will help me reach more heights! How can I forget thanking notionpress who guided me about publishing when I knew nothing !! I would like to thank THE WORDINGS , THE QUILL HOUSE and POETRY WORLD ORG. to give a start to my journey by publishing my creations in the anthologies like THE SHADES OF RAINBOW, ENIGMA VOLUME SECOND,ETC .Hoping for your support throughout the walk.

THANKYOU EVERYONE FOR BEING THERE FOR ME!!!!

1. MASK OFF

Smiles that are spreading around
May have unseen saddest frowns
The loud laughters in those jokes
may have night long miserable groans
The one sweetest with one and all
Is maybe being castigated
The one with always a smile on
From inside is maybe the one worst fated
The one being the most trustworthy
May have gone through demolishing betrayal
The one seeming to be flourishing
May have felt everything but capable!

2. CHANGING SIDES

Not gonna go with the idea of jealousy anymore
Its not what everybody face
Some have to deal with the disturbing crisis of
Being jealous of,lets now go with that type of role in the race
The rosy blooms are no longer pretty
The lilac petals are so exquisite,I'm gonna go pluck one
What does the flower do?
Withstand the wickedness or the pain of separation,
Tell me what should it pursue?
{This stanza aims on the idea that society will have problems with
everything,whether you flourish or you fail.}
Do what you can do best
Their job is to smirk,their job is to say
They'll tease you on what you've achieved
I hope you're getting me
If yes,you ned to move forward
Don't care,Don't hear and let it be!
You can deal with it amazingly
Just think you're of that worth
Just think you've achievd something
That you've changed sides in the crew
And now people are after you!!

3. YOU

Hey!You need yourself and no one else
You'll have problems that will destroy you
You'll lose people,you'll lose trust,you'll be hurt a million times
But remember,you need to keep together yourself for the beautiful future
shines
Hey!Cry and take your time
But not for a long time
You need to get up,you need to start again
Accept it and start moving with a pace,'coz you need to handle
yourself,you are the last and you are the prime
You may lose everyone
You may have trust issues
But don't lose the one,trust that one,have a grip
And my dear that one is just you,yes you!!

4. ONE LIFE, YES ONE!

Make memories, beautiful ones

Enjoy the life, its just a single one

Let the stresses fly away

Dear, why don't you understand?

Its life, only a single one, not like some sport match

Who knows about a second life

Or damn it, even about a second day

Have fun, take the fullest out of the day

As anyone hasn't seen tomorrow

Maybe you'll just be a stationary smiling body in a grave overmorrow!

Have fun, do whatever you want to

Spelling each word correctly W-H-A-T-E-V-E-R

Nothing's kept in being the perfect human in eyes of others

Yes, do good deeds

But make your life the best, the perfect one

So you can say, yes I had a human life once!!

(Don't misinterpret words like 'whatever'. It does not refer to bad deeds or hurtful stuff. Just the perspective of enjoying life. HAPPY READING!!)

5. YOUR SMILES ARE FOR YOU TO LIVE!!

Even more important than getting good from melancholy moments
More essential is taking the fullest out of an amiable day
What is going on, be pleasant, have joys
Forget about what's coming next or what you'll have to deal with later
Remember to live what you now have
This is what life is
Recognize and bless this!!
People forget living good
In worries of some future sorrows
Remember to have a feast with pals now
Worry about the bills after having a joyful feast
Remember this always and forever and,
Forget about tomorrow for today atleast!!
You're jovial, focus on that
Doesn't matter whats gonna come afterwards
Just give your noble smiles a lovely pat
No one's gonna give you reasons to smile truly
You need to hunt and live them yourself for the sake of yourself being
happy!!

6. YOU WILL PASS!!

You are there to fulfil your dreams
Work for them and you'll get flowering success
You are self sufficient already dear
There's just a need for a great push
And you'll reach there !!
Saddest moments will be there
But you'll pass them strongly
Don't fear anything
Be positive and go through it
Don't let your problems guide your strength,Remember to be lit!!
Let your inner strengths and beauty develop
Know your worth and what wonders you deserve
But to get those flourishing desires come true,
You need to overcome those fears,those problems,and that pessimism
Press a halt to every obstacle hurdling your view!!!

7. SELF TRUST

They say life is built on trust
And yes it is!
Just a difference in the two opinions
I say trust you yourself
You'll get a sweet succesful bliss.
Don't doubt yourself
Work on your potential as best as you can
Then let it be,it'll be great,it'll not be a mess
Trust self and you'll do wonders
Be confident that you yourself are enough for your success.
Do what you want to
Do it the way you want
Be satisfied on what you are doing
Relax,work and leave it with trust
Be patient,you're assured to get a peak result.

8. HOPE, A RAY OF LIGHT

Never stop hoping, never be pessimistic
Optimism is the best way of living a good life
I'm not saying saying to hope for fantasy, only the ones realistic!

Never leave hope even when you failed somewhere
Work harder and I promise you
It will be with you it'll be surely there!

Don't worry just give your best and be positive
You'll get a wonderful success dear
I assure you, your will, your hope will be self narrative!

We say where there is a will there is a way
Yes you'll get the perfect road to be there
If you are heartedly hoping, yes hope will prove to be a light's ray!

9. LET IT BE

They'll ask you to go away
To have a chat with someone else
But you can't tell that it did hurt
Due to the fear of losing 'em, creating a permanent uncrossable midway
wall
Once and for all !!
You feel so uncomfortable
You have weary torn nights
But you are stuck midway
You can't end that now
As you know they'll not care and it will end
Everything shattered would there lay
And you'll have no one to get your heart mend!!
You miss those old bonds
When you felt jovial around them
When they chose you over everythng
When it wasn't a sad memory to be around them
But remember, who'll get hurt is you
Who'll be destroyed is you
So don't overthink, try your best
But if it doesn't seem possible to get a way back to'we'
Always remember to LET IT BE!!

10. TRUST HIM

If you are tensed, or you can't choose
Anything is stressing you out and you can't get a way through it
Leave everything to a golden power,
Which is not just in a temple with a priest, its right beside and insid
you, search a bit!!
Trust him, it'll turn out to be great
Maybe he'll do anonym of whatever expectation you do
But trust him more than anyone existing
For sure, it'll be for some good, you'll get a clue!!
Don't shrug for you not being sure
If you trust him, leave it to him
People will smirk, they'll tease
But have patience, once it lits up, it'll not be dim!!

11. THINGS ARE PERFECT NOT PEOPLE

Things are perfect, not people

No one, Yes no one is absolutely perfect

Yeah, it might seem to be so

But believe me they definitely have some hidden scars

Believe me, making mistakes is not a character flaw

You also have a lot in you, work for it and you'll too shine in those stars!!

Its okay not to be best at everything

Its okay to make mistakes

Its a compulsory human trait

Your companion might be so better than you in a field

But remember, He's not you, you're different

Stop comparing your worth, stop caring about the comments

Your true passion is somewhere there, might be concealed!!

Recognize in what you are great

Recognize your worth on that base

Because anyone's life is not perfect

Everyone have their own issues

So stop comparing your strength,

Everyone in their respective chores are on top of the steeple

Remember THINGS ARE PERFECT, NOT PEOPLE!!

12. PATIENCE DOES HAVE SWEET FRUITS

This will be a solution
For if you fail
Just remember you did your best
And that's where necessity lies
In being the best of yourself
You'll one day, assuringly have successful pies!!
Just wait patiently
Don't give up exhaustingly
Don't think your sleepless nights wasted
Remember its only what matters
Wait and struggle again, you'll have your success tasted!!
People have mouths and they will speak
They'll smirk, they'll tease, they'll make you cry whole nights
But listen carefully now,
You have your individual life and its yours
Don't think and move` ahead and force those to scream a loud WOW!!

13. LIVING LIVES

Life is for you to live
To have vital joyful moments
Its what it was created for
To have fun,to have an enjoyable roar
Not for those miserable frowns
Not for the tears shredding
Meet your true self and teach your soul to enjoy
Its what you deserve for your life to be,please don't let it destroy
Take the fullest out of a day
That's what everyone should say
Live the life to its fullest
Happiness is something in your control and you can yourself give
Rmember,life is for you to live!!

14. UNTIL YOU KNOW

You don't know what treasures are there
In a broken scratched weary gate
"It must be and abandoned storeroom"
Wait till the keys of the door
That might be a fabled room or anything more!!
Don't think who's the culprit
Until you know the full tale
Until you know each perspective
Don't judge simply by what they did
Their true character might be forcefully hid!!
A lustrous newly built door though
Lure you into thinking big
When you kick it open though
It might be a few feet space
A dusty old torn one, Just the outer giving it a grace!!
You might be awarding the wrong
Someone else might deserve that
Don't mistaken yourself
Until you know the deepest cause
Until you know who desrves that appreciating pause!!

15. JUST THE WAY YOU ARE

You know what, its about you!
It doesn't matter what people think and say!
You firstly need to love your body
However it is, dark fair, skinny, fat, remember its you
So just be gratful and thanks almighty for your body being this way!!
You need to love your physical self
You need to respect your body
Dear, you need to show everyone
That you love yourself, and you are obsessed with yourself more than anybody!!
Be on a diet, and do exercise
Beecause you wanna be healthy and fit
And no, not because you want to change your state
Not to show someone that you are better now,
Understand, you already were lit!!

16. NOW

Present is the only time
Leave whatever happened yesterday
Whatever will happen tomorrow,dear you'll deal with it
But remember the whole life is in present,thus make it lit!!
You'll ruin your present thus your entire alive time
Thinking,stressing about past or maybe future
Make a goal,work on it with all your power
But firstly its the present you've got,realise and go take a peaceful shower!!
Spread love,happiness,joy and optimism
Not hatred,depression,anger and issues
Let me take some seconds of your stressful life
To make you realise that make yourself truly alive!!

17. PATIENCE IS A BEAUTIFUL WORD

Patience is a beautiful word
A human's most important trait, I would say
Everything takes time, passing of a season or even a single day!
The leaves would fall in autumn,
And the spring grow them gradually with time
Hurrying may lead to a very bad crime!
Patience is a beautiful word,
As impatience may turn stuff topsy-turvy
Learn being patient, I assure you it'll be a beautiful journey!
Being patient is an art in itself
Its not so easy to learn
But believe me, once you learn it you'll never return!
As I say, Patience is a beautiful word!!

18. A PLACE CALLED HOME

Whatever heavens you visit
Whatever palaces you go in
Whatever comforts you get in your pal's place
A place called home is always waiting behind you
Its always standing upright to protect you from wind,enemies,and your
feelings are stuck with it with and adhesive glue!!
Whatever your dream place is
Whatever friends you wanna spend your time with
Whoever people you trust blindly
The people in a place called home will never ever betray you
You need not have a second thought for sharing yourself with your
mom,dad and the brothers too!!

19. OH NO DEAR!!

See that person?His life is amazing
See that one,he has a great luck
Oh damn! I also want to be succesful like that man.
Excuse me! That person has avoided sleeps
And yes,he must have had the worst fate atleast once
Listen!Everyone's got the same amount of potential
Just recognize it soon and go for it,
And you'll one day be that role model!!
No one's got something extra
Or no one's got a moment of the day more than you,
Just you need to trust yourself
And why don't you believe?You'll be there!!

20. MONEY ISN'T THE ONLY WORD

Great and compassionate deeds buy you respect,

Not dollars, yen, or rupee

Don't be greedy for some currency

Earn respect & love, not loads of money

And yes everyone has to agree!

Money can't buy you happiness

It can buy you big houses and pretty clothes with a brand

Earn to make your lifestyle great

But you need to work for your dignity a bit more

And yes then for sure you'll have a life grand!

Have sympathy, and empathy

Have compassion, have concern

Help them, serve them those in need

Have an urge to feel things

Don't be evil, let the hungry ones feed!

21. BEAUTY OF BRAVERY

Thinking about bravery Pictures flash across Mind From flying action heroes
To fake car liftings and the images vary
But brave are people
Ready to give their lives
Oh! what a perfect physique they have
And damn the Elegance of their spirit
Makes me wanna rise up there!!
Captain Vikram Batra sir
An ideal figure of God's art
A figure visual of humanity
A perfect deserver
Of the reverent, high gallantry respect
With heads high and Lifestyle erect!!
Symbolisation of auspiciousness in that green
Their sacrifice is for flag and till the flag
I salute you sir,I owe you a lot, Every Indian bowing to you
I hope someday sometime I would pay
The things you did for us
Hope for all your well being for which I heartedly pray!!

22. DREAMS

Dream dear,you need to dream first
Get up from the couch and work for it
Kick despair away,have a dream and that thirst
Work for it,go ahead!
Show people that the failure hasn't stopped you yet
Work for it with all your potential & you'll be there
I personally bet!!

23. ALONE

You felt that deeply
Those harsh words
Never expected, never thought of
But when that happened
Blurry visions gave you mental thuds!!
You need someone
Not your diary this time
But no one you can trust now
But you can get some help
Oh no one's there for you, irony, wow!!
You'll wet pillows
You'll deal with it
Nothing to choose, You have to
You'll hug a cushion
If no one alive can help you get out of that dark pit!!

24. NOT TO WORRY!

Alot of stuff happening

Really, alot

She just wanna cry

And hug someone but whom??

Her problem is very tiny

Yes she knows

But what can she do she just can't take it

She just wanna be in bed whole day and whole time!!

She tries to be happy

To be engaged

Yes even she is able to

But whenever a thought arises

Ughhh her life is dumpeddd!!

She knows its not such big of a crisis

Maybe its not one for you

But believe me

We all need to handle them

Atleast we should try!!

If we can't do anything now

We must stop those rubbish thoughts arising

We'll see what'll happen

We'll cry later on

Whenever that'll happen!!

Just stop crying now

Stop wasting your days worrying
Maybe I'm not the one to say this
But maybe it'll change someone and make 'em happy!!

25. GLANCE TO OUTDOORS

Pretty high mountains with a sharp peak
Those streams and clean emerald rivers
Butterflies humming around the amiable flowers
Clean blue skies with a shade of light white clouds dispersed.
Small beaks pecking on the seeds
Bare feet crossing the wet green grass
The scene of birds in sky being enthusiastically picturesque
And peaks reaching for the end of sky.
The fresh water falls
With an unknown source last in the hill
The sand,the land and the grass
All being under the feet.

26. YOUR WORTH

Today, a poem to let you know
The true aspect of your life
Its not about worrying all the time
I want you to stop caring
Trust me, you'll get a wonderful lifetime!!
You'll experience all by yourself
You'll deal with alot
From feeling inferior to feeling someone is wrong with me
Care about the people who care about you
Work on the statement and I swear to god
Dear, you'll transform your life and have a real one, you see!!
No one is capable of letting you know your worth
Just you need to know, you desrve a great life
Be wonderful with the people who truly care
Observe and love the real ones mere
Don't give a damn about others
Babe, why do you care so much?
Why do you want everyone
Never give someone the right to hurt you!
You will have a great life since your birth
And thats your worth!!

27. NO ONE TILL THE END

Learn to live on your own
You have to
No one is there till the end
Everyone will leave
if you don't get on what they want
For anyone, you don't have to bend!
No one is there till the end!!
You too have your dignity
You have your pride
You have the worth to be a priority
Just don't forcefully stop someone
Let them go
You have yourself on your side!!
I know separation hurts
I know it does
Those with hours of chats
Now just a smile and walking ahead
Its not just about the love of your life
Be it your buddy, your friend
Be a little selfish, as still, there is no one till the end!!

28. THAT SQUAD

Someone who can be trusted blindly
The people to share everything with
Laughs,talks,fights and what not with them
Oh!The friends,only the true ones,are a true gem!
Humours,secrets everything is shared
Nothing to be kept from those
And frankly speaking of them,
They are the annoying idiots
But no one is as loving as them!
Every decision is collective
In a beautiful pal's squad
Problems are solved in the best of all way
Best part of our lives--Everyone in the world agree and say!!

29. REMEMBER

You will see people laughing at you
Reasons can be varied
They'll judge you, maybe they'll tease
Remember to love yourself with ease..
And that's enough to have a beautiful and sufficient life
Always remember to live a comendable life and remember to survive!!
You grow and you rise upto there,
You'll live your own life
You need to make your life good for just you my dear
Not for anyone existing out there
Remember to live for yourself mere!!
You kick aside all the giant hurdles there
So that you can walk ahead
And As I say
Always remember to live your day!!

30. ISN'T IT AWFUL?

Isn't it awful seeing the people you loved leaving?

Isn't it awful turning your infinite love for someone into hate?

Isn't it awful seeing your luck turning into this fate,

Hey ! Its life it'll be awful but wait

It'll soon turn beautiful!!

Isn't it awful thinking so much about some words?

Isn't it awful seeing yourself crying for someone you thought you'd never?

Listen,no one will be there till the end,none,ever

Hey!Its life it'll have downs but wait

It'll soon be rising!!

Isn't it awful seeing someone going just opposite as you expected?

Isn't it awful hating someone so much you once loved the most?

Isn't it awful having yourself deeply lost?

Hey! Its life it'll be dull and dark but wait

It'll soon turn bright!!

The End

Thank you so much everyone for giving me an opportunity.I hope I'll get a great response from this book.This book was written with a hope to help you. If not help,I hope this must have brought a small smile on your face.You just need to keep yourself together, trust yourself, don't worry, trust your worth and remember to live!!